This Journey Isn't Over Yet

Writings By:
Tommie L. Stanfield, III

To Eddie,

Thank you for the love and support!
You are an amazing creative and
I want you to always remember that!
I really appreciate you!

Copyright Page

ISBN: 979-8-9893436-0-7

Publication Date: 11/03/2023

Release Date: 11/03/2023

Illustrated by Caz'Mier Harris

For more information and other books please visit the websites the below or email the author directly

98_youngthomas@gmail.com

stanfieldtommieiii@gmail.com

Introduction

Following the 2017 release of my Book I, Where To Start, I present my Book II, This Journey Isn't Over Yet. This is a collection of my poetry from over the past few years, taking a deeper dive on experiences of life and looking at different perspectives trying to understand it all. In this life, everything comes around full circle, the past overlaps the present and the future is impacted upon the present. One of the most important ideas is that one shouldn't get stuck in the past because it cannot be changed, instead focus on learning from the experiences and applying the wisdom to your present and future opportunities. Life is about progression and once that's understood, then you will be able to live more for the future; don't let your past create barriers stopping you from doing what you need to do for yourself. We all need to understand, me included, that the present is a gift. I'm still learning not to dwell on the past and to love the present which develops into my future.

"I have great respect for the past. If you don't know where you've come from, you don't know where you're going. I have respect for the past, but I'm a person of the moment. I'm here, and I do my best to be completely centered at the place I'm at, then I go forward to the next place."

- *Maya Angelou*

Table of Contents

This Journey Isn't Over Yet:

I. Looking at the Present

Who I am

I was born into a happy home that was still building
The accidental cherry that made us more appealing
So, let's peel more back to my name, Tommie Lee
My grandfather was the first, so I became Tommie III
The personality of a country boy that was born in the city
My dad's love for music sparked my love for the art
Strumming his guitar, watching strings perform from the heart
I love all periods of music, no matter the place or time
Its just so timeless and honest
And thats what I wanted to do, but life just hit me fast
I knew if I didn't work for it, it wasn't gonna happen or it wasn't gonna last
I had hoop dreams, but I came back to reality
I had rap dreams, but I also wanted a salary
A steady income, I'm thinking, "who could really be mad at me"
Chances were slim already, so I took a different path
Because I didn't work hard enough, I would never push pass the entry level
So I had to take to a new journey, dodging the devil by the grace of God
Following in His footsteps, but always stumbling hard
Living for myself but always living for God
Making decisions based on other people was large for me
Because I wasn't following my own heart, I think I lost it

But, I finally found it when I came back to where I started

I said was, so making my own decisions and dwelling, who I parted with

They weren't in my vision of what I had envisioned so they couldn't fit
And I'm pleased with the people I partnered with
I learned a lot from them as they came and went
Hours spent, talking to my sister about how this life can get
Out of control real fast, so you better get a grip
On to something but it went nowhere fast, it didn't last, find a new path
To be inspired to amplify self-expression, trying to find that one direction
Writing is a way out of everything, but I must go back in
Back to reality, my virtual escape always had to end
Like being outside all day, but when the streetlights came on, I had to go in
The world is full of sin and I'm just trying to stay faithful
Temptations everywhere and I don't understand how to be stable
Thunderstorms everywhere, I don't how to be able
To stand the rain, running wild like horses on the terrain
I wasn't like everyone, there was no ice in my veins
I kept it simple while others were simply running game
Females approach me, but when I to them, most times were in vain
I didn't use to know what a vibe was, so I was looking for acceptance
But then I found myself, now if we don't vibe then I can't mess with
You anymore, random requests will no longer be accepted
Just get, understand, that I am being selfish
Because I'm choosing who I want to be around
But listen, it's the vibe and karma always come back around
That's why I'm cool on people that won't try to fit their crown

I'm laid back to the point where I'm almost touching the ground
I want to stay grounded, but the air is where I can soar
Flapping my wings, sticking my chest out a little more
I know I can score, hitting the three for the game, for my name, feel my pain
Smiling through the history, but what does smiling gain
Smiling through the pain and overlooking the shame
Had a dream that my brother walked out of the hospital in full health
He didn't need any help, but helping me off the couch that I slept on
Family is the foundation of the life that I'm built on
Copying the brick and wood that they have now
Wanting a better life for me, is what they pray for
Always making mistakes and the consequences, I'll have to pay for
But until then, I'll play duty with my brothers, "aye yo, put down the claymore"
8 4, my brother was born and then 8 more years after, my sister came forth
But 2 years prior my other brother was formed and then the baby 8 years later, the star was born

I'm Frustrated

It's so funny but sad, how I'm so easily distracted
Getting caught in the whirlwind or wormhole of social
media
It's hitting all the right spots, so my mind gets greedier
Curiosity is a bitch ain't it, always barking around the
corner to try to get you to look
Every time my phone lights us, I put down this book
My attention was released, and my phone just took,
advantage of me, like come here to mommy and I'm the
baby
It never fails because I haven't turned my phone off lately
Always walking back, I'm not forced so I don't have to
crawl
The world fascinates me like a baby to a dog, chasing after
a ball, but it trips and falls
I'm just laughing so hard and then I see the TV and start
watching it, now the dog feels lonely
Wanting my attention but my attention is phony
"Doesn't know what it wants"
Because it changes so often
So often that this dog starts barking
Trying to get my attention but my mind is stalking
This thing that glistens but puts kids in coffins
Coughing up blood, but these diamonds they're sparkling
They're so bright, that my vision is blurred
So my attention goes elsewhere, man what a shame
Somethings wrong with my mind because it couldn't
choose a lane
I'm trying to go to sleep, but my mind running a mile a
minute
The dog tried, forget it, I'm too far gone for it to stick with
it

With me, it's leaving, like my attention it's seeking
Something new, I'm leaking, intelligence like I'm Eric, they
set a beacon
It's warning me, saying I'm conforming to the normalcy,
with them controlling me
Reading a book, the intelligence is sapped back in like an
odd tree
Then my mind starts running, it never runs out of energy
Like, are you kidding me
At least it's exercising, it's got to stay in shape, got to stay
fit
So my mind will be elsewhere after this poem is over with

Struggling, With Problems, With Reassurance

I'm having growing pains, wishing things would change
In my life, but I'm still in chains, only making change
Compared to the people making bank, while I'm struggling
to fill my tank
Really, don't know what to think
Maybe this world is against me
But I'm just trying to work for my child, putting it simply
"Everything is gonna to be alright" I'm whispering gently
For some reassurance, because my husband is gone on
another deployment
While I'm jumping from job to job praying for long term
employment
I really hope this next one is a hit
"I'm sorry baby, I just don't have time for it"
Time is a luxury and I have so many responsibilities, I
don't know if this life cut out for me
I mean, I don't think I'm cut out for this life
What do you want from me?
I'm doing all I can, but problems always seem to arise
Out of the ground, like "surprise, I'm going to be sticking
around
For a while, but don't worry because I've got style
So if you want to pop like Drake, I can calm that down
But you can't relax now, you got responsibilities to take
care of"

If you let me, I can pray for you
And watch God do what you know He can do
I'm just trying to look out for you, but if you don't want the
help
I can deal with that too, I'm just trying to give you a clue, a
hint

A message that I sent, but you didn't receive
I guess it didn't process because you didn't believe
In what I'm trying to tell you, I need to understand
Let me delve through your pain
I know you feel like you're in chains, but let me be the change
I'm trying to help you so you won't feel like this again

I don't need your solution, just listen to my pain
You're trying to fix something that just can't be tamed
Life isn't something you can just change in an instant
Life makes people feel alone and distant because of these things, that take so much time
Leisure is just a figment of my imagination
Peace is what I'm chasing but chasing me is life or devastation
I'm slow to trust life, so there's always hesitation
But my pain is too much right now, I'm just so complicated
I don't know how you stick around for me, I feel like I am hated
By everyone, son of a gun, the unlucky one

But you're not, I'm here for you, to listen and to help in any way I can
Just let me help, I encourage and love you, I'm your number one fan
I can babysit while you're working because I can't continue to watch you like this because we are friends
That means that you can trust me like I'm your kin
I'm here for you, in case I need to remind you again
A friend that is a phone call away but please don't pretend, like we don't go way back
There's no way you can forget that
History that is made and formed all through the grades

And college, gathering knowledge, and grad school
And thinking of the man you married, he was mad cool
But military is where his heart truly is, trying to fight for
his wife and his kid
Protecting has always been his strong suit, working hard to
keep his family afloat
Because the boat was approaching the drop, but he made
sure his family was straight and never flopped
But struggling is a part of life in case you forgot
It's normal, you just have to stick it out and keep rowing to
avoid the drop

Measurement of a man

What's the measurement of a man
What ruler do you use
Is it all about physicality or the mental capacity
The audacity of them to say anything, they're always
harassing me
Saying "you could never be a real man, you still a baby"
Then I list my accomplishments and they pull out every
excuse from A to Z
Man, forget what they're saying and they expectations,
they don't make you
Instead they take from you, stapling you to a contract that
wasn't made by you
It was made for you, by someone that doesn't have the
same potential as you
By someone who doesn't want to see you follow through
By someone who has never made it to where you're trying
to get to
Don't let people measure your manhood by their opinions
of pretty good

Everybody is created equal

That's a nice sentiment, but nobody really believes it
Always saying one is better than the other, people started
to believe it
They are only taking sides because of what they hear
Their knowledge comes from their ears while others come
from their eyes
Witnessing, white people crippling black people, "not
listening"
We're kneeling, get up!
We're sitting, get up!
We're standing, sit down!
Before you get put down, like the animal you are
They stomp they foot down so we know they mean
business
We politely decline, then get reclined, while the world is
our witness

Wake up

People don't understand the complexity of our complexion,
it's too complex for you to digest
I'll digress
They don't know that he rose from the ground to become a
hero, even though they treated him as zero
What's next
This generation needs to generate the same energy before
we all disintegrate, hating each other so we discingrate one
another
This nation is like none other, that's why we're in
desperate need of exfoliation because this country is an
implosion waiting to happen
But all we hear are condoms breaking, booty shaking,
words from satan, constant stressing, and money regression
I think it's time for progression, where we progress
mentally regress on negative tendencies
Avoid avoidable injuries, show sympathy
The symptoms that are down this path are bringing
negative energies, not meant for me

The trauma that they're having is caused by mental abuse
Abusing the abuser isn't something that Martin Luther
lived for
You know what you could do, is start to give more
For starters, it's important that you start with advantages
By reading for information and not only on college
campuses
We camp out for hours for technologies and other materials
But won't take the time to read up on vitamins and
minerals
It might seem minor, but we need to get to the bottom of
this

What we put in our bodies, that affects the top to the
bottom of us
Really no need to rush, cause time is on our side like the
father is one of us

Instead of minding your own business, let's start by
owning a business and be in a giving mood like you getting
ready for Christmas
Are we on your wish list
We need more than good report if you didn't actually know
We insist on showing support so you letting these people
know, that we back in business
But not for long if you don't use your purchasing power
Now we're out of business so whites continue to devour
And own us
But we're too worried about clapbacks and boners that
we're not doing our job, so don't think you getting a bonus
At least you got a job and you're not homeless
Let's just say we put our priorities on the wrong things
It's like we're trying to give life to something that's
already dead
It's like we're trying to put a bandage on somebody that's
already bled out
He's no longer bleeding but you're still trying to address
the wound
Instead of trying to figure out what to put on his tombstone
Trying to find the better half of his two tones, light or dark,
let's flip a coin
It's not two sided so should you talk about the time where
he used his head or was just acting an ass
It's hard to grasp the cycle that's put in a black man's path
Cause cops are shooting niggas, that's in their path
And niggas shooting niggas over a look…
Then blast

This Journey Isn't Over Yet

Hang time

This isn't only about punchlines and hang time
But it's also about punchlines and hang time
From taking your last punch and taking your last breath
Laying there unrecognizable with no air up in your chest
Body disfigured with rope imprints around your neck
That was my brother but it's nothing left for me to check
We used to hang out, now he's hanging in front of me
Yeah, their uncle, but I got to hide the kids so they can't
see
That if you throw punches, they'll hang you from a tree

Blind

An eye for an eye right
But when looking back on it, was that the right thing to do
in hindsight
Or would you do it again to where you have no sight to
where you can't see the signs
Who would you expect to follow you when your blind
Or would your followers take their eyes out too, so it's the
blind leading the blind
Leaving nobody able to see the sunshine
But wait, is that a crime, keeping everybody equal to be on
the same playing field
Where none can catch or throw because they can't see what
they're doing
Only listening for directions to point them in the direction
of the way to go
Lead us, but you don't know because you're just blindly
walking
Scared out your mind when the leader's no longer talking
But still scared because your leader's continually barking,
out orders
But in order to save a life, you got to be able to save your
own
But nah, forget that, just follow orders and you'll be just
fine
Even if you can't see, it's only a matter of time, before you
reach the destination
Just follow, no hesitation, but they never seen it coming, an
ambush was waiting
Now think about the picture that was just painted, but you
couldn't actually paint it
Visualize what their seeing, darkness, they start believing
that if they can't see it, it's artless, no longer beautiful

Having somebody describe something using words you
don't see fit
So you're blindly searching for words that your sight
usually could get
They think it looks good but you would normally see
otherwise
But now you have to believe it, because you can't see with
your eyes

Rafters

Think about what you're about to do
Think it through, get it through your head that this might
not work
"But doing one job isn't going to be enough
And getting one job isn't going to do it either"
So you're making money fast and blowing it like a sickness
Don't get caught because your downfall will be a witness
You don't want to go to jail, so your death is something
your family will have to witness
But, with your whiteness, you'll go free
No questions asked or piss tests
While we're stressed out, no room to breathe because the
cops pressed
Against us like a painting on a wall
But you know who's hanging, is that even a question at all?
Putting the nail higher and higher, until we can't touch the
ground
Watching the body as it falls, when it hits, don't hear a
sound
But you're thinking job well done, one more down, a
million more to go
I only used 20 bullets this time, next time I'll shoot some
mo
Even when he's down, I got to kick him to make sure
I got to stand my ground against blacks, huh, you know
I want to go back to old days to see how
They whipped them back in shape, thinking, I could've
been fowl
I see them fight all the time, and I would've never called a
foul
I'll just hang them like a jersey in the rafters so everyone
can see

That this man was only a man, the only thing alive is his
legacy
Dang… that means he's no longer on the field to retrieve
for entertainment
I mean, it's just another form of enslavement, I mean
engagement
To connect all the fans to watch the athletes

Don't Forget

I want to enlighten you with something that will spark
through you like lightning
When you see that light, spring into action because this
picture frightening
Save a life to make your life better for your offspring
All spring I'm thinking that I really want to know the
reason why people bring negative comments to positive
situations
When it's passed off to their offspring, parents that are
coughing can't bring them "wisdom" anymore because
they're in a coffin
Costing many more lives to be ruined often
Now listen, teach morals that will develop the mind for the
thoughts to corral and then mull it over
You have no cover, so you have to dodge the bullets of life
that come at you
Thoughts and movements need to be quick, don't be a
statue
Because you need to teach them about melanin and how
racism can come at you
And that you shouldn't conform into anything they throw at
you
No category can contain you, us, we, I
We don't want it anymore so they rebuy and reboot
something that we already did to become fly
I am fly, you are fly, and you have wings so don't let them
make you think you can't fly
I want to see you soar high, spread them wings, make them
see your belly because they're under you
Pride and arrogance are terrible traits that might ruin you
It'll have people flocking to you for the wrong reasons
Or migrating elsewhere, they're all leaving

So the best choice is to stay humble and keep seizing, the moment
Take your time and remember to keep breathing
Because they're counting on you to keep away the all the demons

Utopia

Let me tell you about the world that I'm living in
There's no synonym for this life that I'm imagining
There's plenty of women friends but more importantly, I got family here
In my neighborhood, there is no hood or suburb, we're all living good
There is no poverty, so money doesn't define your property
We all have some type of desire to be a philosopher, something like Socrates
So we'll properly challenge ideas, probably with discussions
No guns bussing, we stay safe like babies under covers
No need to be undercover because morality and honesty is something that everyone has discovered
And follows, no longer flying hollows burying themselves in bodies
Leaving sorrow buried in bodies related to the fallen soldiers
I mean, I told ya, I want black people to become closer
We know our roots and history instead of it being buried under boulders
The formal name is tombstones, but without all this suffering would there even be blues songs
So would the story of the come up be obsolete
But at least everyone would have accessible shoes to put on their feet
Victory is not always, we all shall feel defeat
But never feel defeated, energy is everlasting, it will never be depleted
Only positive vibes to vibe out to, let's ride out to
The things thats on your mind, and I'll share mine too

Dreams of becoming what you want to be and the journey you'll have to live out through
In this euphoria, things won't come easy, there will be work to do
Upon reflection my Utopia is far from perfection but it would be nice to be free of depression
The ills of illnesses shall be eliminated, free glasses of lemonade made by yourself because there are no maids
Everyone is living their dream and getting paid for it
Living in dream homes and they didn't even have to slave for it
But work still needs to be done, you got to teach your sons and daughters
How mothers and fathers are supposed to get along
It's okay to make mistakes just know that some consequences will tag along
People know right from wrong so there won't be any jail time
And everyone's in their right mind
Everyone is the same color, black, so there is no discrimination
And we can all sit down and have complex conversations
Sparking ideas to clash, causing arguments, but then we'll see each other's side causing no complications
I mean, it's just a conversation
There is no time wasting, the doctors got the answers and the cures, we just need to find some patience
So we can be their patient
Health care is not a thing because everyone is entitled to benefits and can fit in this
Category of doctors that helped prevent some of the saddest stories
And lastly, all glory to God for painting this beautiful picture for me…

This Journey Isn't Over Yet

Unraveling

Would you mind if I painted this picture in your mind
Let's say in every single line lies your prescription
And I'm not gone say nothing corny like "you're my addiction"
But just listen
Everybody can see your physical features but what about the mental
I don't want to mess up your mind, so let me be gentle
Let me write your story in pencil so I can erase when you mess up
And I know how you love to get dressed up
So let's get dressed up and go out
Take you on a date so we can show up and show out
Even though other people's opinions don't matter
But it's still kind of nice to hear them chatter
But back to you
Where does God stand in your life
I want to meet your family, I just hope they don't bite
I never really understood that, I don't expect humans to, but dogs just might
When would you let go and when would you choose fight
What and who are you closest to
What would you do if your boyfriend cheated on you
Would you let him have it and forgive or let him go so you can live
If he messes up, would you create a big scene and a big story
So you tell everybody "I got him together" so you can get the glory
Are you searching for fools gold
Or are you gold searching for a fool
That is using you as a tool, but you refusing to leave

Do you like men that have the persistence of Steve
Even though you bash him time and time again, what do
you really have up your sleeve
If you have nothing to hide, then go sleeveless
On Sunday's, do you go to church and praise Jesus
If we actually do this, God is the only one that can get
between us

Taking a Chance

"No ill intentions but I need to mention, the way you looking, really caught my attention
Even though I'm speaking now, when you speak, I'll be attentive, I'm here to listen
I'm not going to objectify you, I want to testify on your behalf
Saying you're more than half, a whole woman, that requires equal cash
I know I'm speaking like I know you when I don't and I'm speaking fast
Enough of me, let me give you the wheel so you can just hit the gas"

I don't know what say, I should just ask for his number
And give the wheel back to him and hit him later this summer
Or respond now to let him know I'm interested
What he said was so intricate
I don't know how to respond
But wait, let me think, is he really for real
Does he really want to know what I think and would I've had to deal with
Or is he just interested in my body that he can have real quick
Is he really interested in my mind, what I have to say and what I'm thinking
Or is he trying stall to figure out what I'm drinking, so he can buy more for his entertainment
What is your definition of ill intentions
Because I need to mention that playing me for a fool is apart of that definition

I don't need defamation of my reputation because I have plenty hating
Let me think...
Okay, let's say I do give him my number
What will he do with it, is he gone hit me immediately, constantly wanting to talk to me
Or will he give me space and show that he doesn't want all of me
But what if that's the best he got, and after it's just dead
Thinking he would've been about more by what he said
Would he leave me on read, well, life is about chances, so here's what I said…

Young King

You're doing too much talking, young king
Have patience when you speak, you'll reach your peak
soon
Just keep playing peak a boo with your son
A young prince not yet in search of the right princess
He'll appreciate the speech when he understands later
You'll teach your son that every single one isn't right for
him
Go left and don't turn back or you'll be frozen
Leaving your place of zen because you couldn't let it go
With it being so cold, it just continued to snow
Muster up enough energy to just say no, before you get too
old
Times up, but let's rewind back when the wind blew strong
And life was simple and sweet, on those warm spring days,
you would go to the beach
Get wet, have fun, take a shower then eat
That moment came when you seen her, you know that
meant something
Her waist was so thin and her body was something
Yall would stay up on the phone and have conversations
about nothing
Having sensations of hitting a home run or just sliding into
second
If she gave you a few seconds, would you break her record
Consistency is what you want, but she was hesitant
She couldn't stay in the tent, she was eighteen looking for
herself, but you weren't content
You didn't look at the context, you were in a contest with
her, looking for her heart
She tried to tell you were going too fast, so everyone's a
shedding a tear

You didn't hear a ding, saying that you were getting near
The edge but you drove off screaming Geronimo
Here we go, it just hit the fan but you forgot, so you're finding Nemo
She's gone forever, you should've fed her instead of your ego
You ever think why she left, she was shooting paintballs and you were shooting torpedoes
Turning up and not listening, she was pregnant, turning nineteen, she about to have a kid soon
You stepped to her plate, hit the homerun all the way to her bedroom
Got pass home plate, the passion gave one point
One son, that's one love, make sure you care of him
Because he's a young prince not yet in search of a young princess
He'll appreciate the speech when he understands later
You'll teach your son every single one isn't right for him
Let your actions speak so you're not talking too much, young king

You See a Queen

Heavy is the head that wears the crown
Quote meant for a King but she's more than worthy
Because she takes care of hers while it's still early
Then takes care of her village, making sure it's not dirty
But always clean
Question, when are you going to realize when you look in
the mirror, you see a Queen
The clear reflection of the robe while holding a flower
Saying you can still do more and never cower
But stand tall at all times
Making sure you still shine
The greatest of all time
Yeah, you're mine
Always on my mind
You're my breath of fresh air, when I take a breath
You're my good night's sleep, when I lay to rest
There is no other, that can wear the crown
There is no other, that can wear that gown
Not quite like you
I got to give credit, when credit is due
I wish you could see things, from my point of view
So you could see what I see, when I look at you
You're like royalty, so you're a Queen
You're like a painting that I've never seen
Only using earth tones for the seams
And everything in between
I'm here for late night calls, when you want to talk
I'm down to go to the park, when you want to walk
I am here with the light, in case things get dark
And you will do the same for me, ready with the spark

Momma

I see you struggling
I'm here to let you know that I'm here for you
Even though you hold it in, I really care for you
I should get on my knees more to say more prayers for you
Sometimes, we take you for granted
And your answers are not always straight, they're
sometimes slanted
To avoid saying what you really feel
Keeping a distance from your emotions until you're alone,
then you let it spill
I know how you really feel
Rarely has tears ever dropped but I am like you and I'm
putting you on a pedestal
And trying to walk with God like you, and listen whenever
He wants us to be still
Mom, I know you are tough as steel and sharp as nails
You always looking after your children, making sure they
prosper and never fail
You make things like a fairytale, to where we felt safe even
though it was craziness outside
Always had us protected with the whole armor of God on
all sides
From the top of our heads, to the soles of our feet
Always showed us the right direction, so we wouldn't
repeat our old mistakes
Or your old mistakes

Appreciation (60)

Just a small demonstration of an illustration that I have for the one I'm facing
First and foremost, I'm glad that I got to keep you in my life
Secondly, you taught me family is important and that showed tonight
All the support you received and all the support that you give
Makes me want to live like you, with a few minor tweaks
Showing my family that it's not only about what you think, it's how you speak
Showing off to everyone and saying you can do this in your sleep
Thirdly, I want to keep your peace, a piece of mind and a mind that's at peace
I'll keep a piece of you in my heart
Fourthly, style is for the young
When you were young, you were fly, I guess over the years someone has been clipping at your wings
Fifthly, you taught me music and how to get into the swing of things
Listening to old music and hearing your guitar and the melody
Thinking I got to get into this music heavily
Listening to the songs he played while talking about the history, he was telling me
The importance of this music and how's its better than today, I see
Where he's coming from but also where this music is going to
Sixty, I mean lastly, we appreciate the wisdom, the tough love, the loud laughs, the true history

You can multiply the love by 10

Stan(d)field

In 1850, in Humboldt, Tennessee, Alex Standfield was
born
A great black man was going to take on Mississippi by
storm
From slavery in Tennessee, to a planter and master
craftsman
Got married to Matilda, started a farm, ten kids, all a part
of the game plan
With incredible courage and perseverance, he built what he
had from the ground
Forged his legacy in stone for future generations,
everything isn't as perfect as it sounds
One of his children, Albert Ross, had a baby that passed as
an infant
I know they wish that things were different
But that didn't stop him and his wife, Zelda, from trying
again until they had six more
One of which is my grandfather that I'm named after,
Tommie Lee, so I'm Tommie III
Strong family, so when you say Stanfield, think free
My roots run deep in this country, within this tree, it's a lot
of company
This family bond is never broken, praise God for being
together
Back to where we started in this country, with love from
me to you, and you, and you
I'm glad we're all showing exactly what this family could
possibly do

Slowly Working

Didn't know what's going on, got the call, there's
somethings wrong
Got in the car, mom was driving, man that ride was mad
long
Jumped out quick, they jumped too, and ran for my life
I got in the door, I wished I would've ran for his life
Because he's lifeless, it's a crisis, I'm praying that Christ is
In the mist, He didn't miss, my brother's helplessness
He helped him up, off the ground, to reverse my
breathlessness
Breakfast is, in the morning, will join us guess again
I'm trying to get, through the nurses, let me know he is
In perfect health, I haven't dealt, with this here, I need
some help
Waiting room's, uncomfortable, they need some better
seats
It didn't matter, too much happening, to even go to sleep
Didn't go in the room, just knew that he's okay
Got updates from the fam, progression was being made
Moving some, it wasn't fun, I hate the hospital
I walked in, he looked at me, I looked at him, I had to leave
Tubes were all, in his mouth, in his arms, I was out
Seeing him, in this way, I couldn't do, so I'll pray
Father, Father, help him please, get him strong, so we can
leave
On His time, not on mine, I forgot, take Your time
Physical therapy, slowly working, he's frustrated, it's not
working
On His time, not on yours, he forgot, he's sorry Lord
I don't know, what to say, to him now, it'll be okay
I don't have a strong suit, not a hero, I can't do
I'm like a straw hat now, they walk pass, I fall down

He hasn't really grown much, he wants to move, dude just
slow down
Check the date, do the math, it's only been a month now
Hard work and perseverance, the only things that'll work
now
Including prayer, thank the Savior, for giving you your life
again
In due time, you'll shine again, keeping on going, no
panicking

Denpoet

He wrote about his struggle, his journey, his love, and his
dreams
He's always been with us, he never switches teams
He stays true to his poetry
Well because he is poetry
It is one with him, so he just let it take control and write for
him
But using his mind that may take him on a whim
His poetry is so influential like Stevie is to him
So I began my journey into writing
He helped me to understand that I should just let it go
instead of fighting
I let it control me and now I can't stop writing
5 books with 70 plus in each book
His mind is so complex, thoughts he just lets them cook
And the product is as pure as a great poet
Which he is
So it's nothing I can say but I'm glad that he's my brother
He helped me enter this realm of poetry that I think no
other could
Will I be able to get through the trees of his mind or be lost
in the woods?

Von Graves

He went on a journey with his passion in a pen
No knowing when but he knew he was going to win
Going to be something that everyone wants to see
Performing in front of thousands and touching each
individually
But that's just a start
He is just a small flame now
But just wait until later when he burns the whole place
down
Moms and pops are both proud
To see how far he's came and where he will go
Inspiring all people and controlling the crowd
With his lyrics to show that his mind is more than profound
His insight is so out of sight that people can't understand it
yet
His vision goes beyond music
Creating different ideas so they influence
Other people to think more, plan more, and take action
To come up with more ideas and stop acting
Like you're doing it yourself when you're really not
Be like Von Graves that's Fearless and about control the
spot
Make big dreams and pursue them cuzzo
The sky is never the limit so all you got to do is go

Best Friend

What is the point of having a best friend, just to talk to?
Are they helping you out with your game, like a walk
through?
It's more about advice and then having fun
There should be chemistry
I don't need nobody to pity me
My best friend looks out for me
Making sure I'm good and encourages everything I'm about
to be
And it's vice versa, I make sure she's good constantly
Well, at least I try, but she's better than me
She cares more while dealing with her own things
We already are champions, but we're looking for more
rings
Making sacrifices for the betterment of the team
You enter that team when a bond is formed
That friendship needs to be strong where it can't be torn
We listen the Joey, sometimes land of the free
Trying to not to freeload or be dead in the street
Always praying for each other's safety from the top of our
heads to the soles of our feet
There are friendships formed with everyone we meet
But there is a special bond between two best friends that
can't be beat

Musical Geniuses

I'm sticking to my Roots and I'm on the Quest for Love
Keeping my Thoughts Black and my heart on my sleeve
And a Q Tip in my Eardrum, Phife why you had leave
I Wonder if people would take me As I Am, if I tried to
play Keys
Or should I use 808s to cure my Heartbreak, now wait
You can't tell I can't step to the plate, I'm just trying to
make it to Heaven's gates
Maybe I can use this Coloring Book to paint a way
What if I make a Soul Tape but is that like Sailing My Soul
But I'll keep it Trapped only for God to get to
Until he takes it, I'll keep my Sight High for the Prince in
order to get in the Kingdom
Let him come into your heart and guide you through the
Blueprint
I'm too lit, bringing the Culture with me, I'm like a
toothpick
Riding this raging bull at this Rodeo, it's stupid
I should be riding this Everlasting Wave instead
Getting ahead, I'm trying to stay Ill, keeping it autoMatic
in my head
I need some bread, where is Niko and Brutus
Probably up to no good, man these dudes are foolish
I'm currently on the Low End and nobody has a Theory to
get me out this slump
I felt like I've been dumped, when Things Fall Apart, there
no one to Pump, me Up
Until you came around, trying to teach me how To Pimp A
Butterfly, but I don't understand The Technique
If you switched up the plan, I wouldn't be so nervous, be
Sweating everywhere thinking bout closing the curtains
I don't want No Problems and that's for certain

But I'm Surfing The Internet, gathering knowledge so I can interject
The teacher isn't telling the whole story, we've all been Miseducated
Don't blame her, she doesn't know the things that has never made it, to the history books
So I'll teach myself by my listening to Laila's Wisdom
Even though it pains me like I just pulled it out, I got to listen
To the whole thing, but it's gone be Alright
Because I came to find out we're worth more than 24k gold
I can't believe this 6lack Magic was sold
I'm not a Savage but I will come back Without Warning
Back To Black, like I never left to go back to touring
So I Decided, I want to talk less About Nothing, and More about these people that are constantly struggling
I'm not even all that Thirsty, but I'll drink water anyway
But it's people that only drink once every 48 hours or two days
Indulging in this Food and Liquor, they need Food and Liquor II
Everybody don't know what this Food and Liquor can do
For your soul, these mind games enhancing your brain but killing your liver
Deliver these lines, it's only a matter of time before I go Off The Wall
And come for your head like Django Jane, they put multiple Chainz on my body but can't chain my mind
Because it's out of the Boxx they tried to put it in, you can't adjust my Speaker, you just have to take it in
Listen to it once, and then listen again, catch everything because it's coming fast like the city of winds
Commonly, I use to think about where we would begin…

This Journey Isn't Over Yet

This Journey Isn't Over Yet:

II. While Reflecting on the Past.

Lost Love

When I look into her eyes
I see everything
Her past
Her present
Her future
Assembling the pieces that were broken to understand the
whole perspective
Overwhelmed with the amazing life that I get to observe
But I'm done being a spectator
I'm trying to show you the whole spectrum of what we can
build
There is nothing we can't do, we won't let a game
determine which block is going to make us fall
Because we are consistently reinforcing structures that we
created
The creator would be pleased, giving the best of ourselves
to others in order to cure this disease of
...
Lost love

F.

1. People say catching *feelings* is a disadvantage
2. It's not that it isn't advantageous but you can get caught with your pants down
3. So you get embarrassed, but wear it proudly
4. Because only *fools* let that get to them
5. But *fear* is something that is unavoidable
6. Something you can't get around
7. The only way is through, so we have to become *fighters*
8. So we can break through to obtain our *freedom*
9. With that, build a *foundation* that your legacy will be built on
10. *Forget* all the people that don't believe in you
11. Your legacy will live on through your children and many more generations
12. It starts with catching *feelings* and seizing the moment

O. O.

1. He *often operates* on feelings without a shadow of doubt in mind
2. He knows she's the right choice, it's only a matter of time
3. Before she sees it too, in her mind
4. I mean she *originally omitted* the thought of love, crossed it out her mind
5. She *often omits* the whole idea of catching feelings
6. She forced it out of her mind, but with him, it was different
7. She couldn't help herself, she *often operates* on the thought of being isolated
8. Meaning they wouldn't even had the chance but he *originally offered* many things
9. His *opportunities offered* her a home, a partner, a family, and later on a wedding ring
10. She began to ignore the *outrageous opinions* of doubt that her mind would bring
11. They both had the thought they would they go to infinity and beyond
12. Letting those thoughts *overstay, often* creating a peace of mind

L.

1. They knew it was *love* and none could tell them otherwise
2. They have that type of bond that you thought will never break
3. Always there for each other on time, they were never late
4. *Love* was always on time, when it was needed, it would show its face
5. Because it's needed in *life*, to give to his wife, along with other things
6. His nights would stay bright, alongside his woman laying down
7. They didn't take *losses*, it was unheard of until now
8. They would start changing, growing apart as *life* went on
9. Their *legacy* was no more, they split as far as the moon to the sun
10. Without *loyalty* in the relationship, they could've never won
11. Now it's over, just as fast as it had begun
12. But still deep inside there are feelings, *lingering*, that can't be outrun

Hurting

How can I lose something so precious to me
There's nowhere I need to be, except right here with you
But your gone, so what am I supposed to do
I thought I seen you, I need to get to you, I need to keep
pushing through
This crowd but you foul because you kept moving too
I'm chasing a memory, a part that I liked but not the whole
you
Now I realize, I only catered to a part of you, so you
departed from me
Leaving with a part of me that I won't get back
That you'll soon part with, leaving it somewhere out of
your mind
So you can move on
With someone else, while I try to find myself
Recreating the part that you took from me
I should call someone because there was a burglary
You stole something from me then left it somewhere I
couldn't see
So I couldn't find it
Maybe you still got it but it's in bondage
Trapped but ingrained inside you like a traumatic
experience
Trying hard to tell it to get out, but it's not hearing you
Not understanding this, language that you speak of
What is get out, she must mean stay in
Women never know what they want, they always playing
Playing with emotions, showing false devotions, not
interested in you but what you holding…

How can you lose something so precious to you

There's nowhere you need to be, except right here with me
But I'm gone, so what are you supposed to do
You thought you seen me, you need to get to me, you need to keep pushing through
This crowd but I'm foul because I kept moving too
You're chasing a memory, a part that you liked but not the whole me
Now you realize, you only catered to a part of me, so I departed from you
Leaving with a part of you that you won't get back
That I'll soon part with, leaving it somewhere out of my mind
So I can move on
With someone else, while you try to find yourself
Recreating the part that I took from you
You should call someone because there was a burglary
I stole something from you then left it somewhere you couldn't see
So you couldn't find it
Maybe I still got it but it's in bondage
Trapped but ingrained inside me like a traumatic experience
Trying hard to tell it to get out, but it's not hearing me
Not understanding this, language that I speak of
What is get out, he must mean stay in
But men always know what they want, but never telling
Never telling emotions, showing false devotions, not interested in you but what you got...

No way out

Don't take this personal
But personally, I'm not close to you
What do I do, grow closer to myself
I need the space if you don't get it
You'll get it eventually
Mentally, I feel like this lonely life is meant for me
Not feeling down on myself, it just what it is
I am what I'm not
Tying a tight knot around my neck with my tie
Taking my business elsewhere, I'm leaving so goodbye
To you and yours as I enter into my own space
Covering the footprints in the sand, don't want anyone to
trace
Me, because I'm going in the water
Drowning with these thoughts in my mind
Trying to find myself in this wild sea, while it's cloudy
Don't tell me you were in the water, I said don't follow me
She couldn't hear, like there was bad quality
Let me see if I can lose her in the air
I'm trying to dodge all this negativity because it's pollution
If they struck a fire, my mind might flair up into flames
What a shame, she caught a plane, following me again
Let me try this quicksand and maybe she would quit then
But my mind started sinking, panicking, got to think quick
man
But when I tried to get out, I seen she was pulling me in
Thinking she would win, but superhero movies always has
a happy ending, so I'm not going out like this
If there were snakes all around, I would grip tight like this
Then quickly release when I'm out of the predicament
Because I used you, but I don't want you to use me

So now I'm hiding in the grass, thinking that she would
pass me
How fast she's moving, I would think that she's an athlete
Found me, grabbed me by my arm and dragged me
Now I'm stuck in the mud, while it's still raining, I just
hope I don't drown
And now I can't breathe, it's like she's got me pinned down
I just need to find a way to get away

Hiatus

He went on a hiatus and it was quite contagious because he
couldn't stay away
Trying to stay mentally stimulated so his mind wouldn't
fade away
Because his mind was so complex that with his canvases,
they couldn't take the paint away
Painting use to take the pain away but it stopped so he had
to break away and escape
To a faraway island, he laid, writing the pain away
But the pen burst, so the ink sprayed, painting a picture like
a vision
The idea hit him like a head on collision, so he decided to
make a decision
To follow his epiphany, after achieving each goal, he heard
a sweet symphony, letting him know, he's going in the
right direction
Upon reflection, he dissected his rejections and collected
them to create perfection

COLOURS

Everybody, everybody, listen up
I want to tell yall a story
How I met this one girl and I swear she was meant for me
I like the way that she moves
And she was just so smart but back to the way she moves,
it was like art
It's in her hip
The way she do her dance and the way she dip
I'm trying not to trip
Last thing is her lipstick
It's a dark red color, man she's so sick
Okay I lied because she was killing em with them lady
pants
She put me in a trance
Then she looked at me and smiled when I glanced
So she waved me over for a dance and I decided to take a
chance
As we both started to dance, we started sweating crazy
I was thinking we need a fan
We was heating up the room but we need to cool off
sooner rather than later
I think we need paper, towels or something
She like that I was real because other dudes be fronting
The music stay bumping, booming through the bass now
The way she moving I'm saying baby don't stop now
After a while, she went to the bathroom but ended up
leaving the building
Man, how she slipped through my fingers like that
I ended up seeing her a week later in the same place,
thinking about approaching her but I would be in the
wrong
But man, my mind spaced when I heard this song

Everybody, when this song came on, I finally realized after a while
I wanted to be apart of the Cool Outrageous Lovers Of Uniquely Raw Style

SpottieOttieDopaliscious

My SpottieOttieDopaliscious
Giving her a million kisses
Million tries, I got persistence
Got help, I need assistance
Need forever, always Mrs.
Always ready, no resistance
Nothing less you're so delicious
Damn
I need a breath to talk about my angel in disguise
Sometimes she's hard to recognize
But when I sing lullabies in her left ear, I hear her moan
and cry
Hearing them play our song in her right ear
Living in the moment that's right here
Right now
I would serenade her, let it marinate while I was gone and
came back with her wanting another plate
I was never late, we would gravitate closer because
conversations made us elevate
Higher in knowledge, always learning, we'll never graduate
I'm always hungry, I'll always grab a plate
Don't fall for traps because they're in their place
Always disguised as something else, they'll never show
their face
Until they get what they wanted then they just want their
space
I thought we were growing closer but it was really apart
Damn
Separation consumed us, creeping more with every
moment
She wanted atonement, I wouldn't condone it
All I can do is hope for a better day

But I remember like it was yesterday
When I hear those horns, I'm thinking "they're playing our song" usually
When it was you and me, thinking how it use to be
Crucially, I lost you, in the process I made a fool of me
You're with everyone else and I'm just the Outkast
Damn

Motion picture

She's a work of art
The work of the greatest artist
The way she moves is just poetry
See if she would notice me, being a small picture in her
large canvas
I mean, the world is her campus
Where she's continuing to learn this art of poetry
She's holding the strings, steadily controlling me
As she walks, the frame moves with her
As she speaks, the camera picks up the dialogue
As she performs, the audience feels her presence
Because she's a present in a form of a paper and an easel
Expressing her thousand words, making her present good
versus evil
She's never see through, you see what she draws or paints
Showing her triumph and failures, pains and pleasures, and
all of the treasures
Showing that she's just like you, through the sketches
Even though she's strong, she's fragile, almost paper thin
You can rip right through her with your hands, if she lets
you in
Breaking a whole sculpture into two halves, if she's lucky
Because she could be in pieces
Trying to find a way to carve happiness in hard times
When she does her thing, you can see her heart shine
As she paints and sips this glass of fine wine
Even though she doesn't have the full figure, but she'll age
like fine wine
When she paints, time flies
Started in the morning and when finished, she sees night
skies
Engulfed in her art, to say the least

When she's angry, she paints like a savage beast
And when she sleeps, she sees the patterns and the
movements of the one she seeks
And when she weeps, she uses colors that can convey how
she's feeling
Painting for herself to release these feelings
Loud expression, instead of snapping at these villains
Not for money, but she's trying to make a killing
Not for fame, she wants to stay underground
But her rail rose to the surface
She had support and now she supports others
Even the red, white, and blue and all of the other colors
She paints pictures that's always in fluid motion
And rowing this boat all over the ocean
Exploring everywhere that her mind can think of
Exploring all the aspects of motion picture and she's on the
brink of
More creation, contemplating, no hesitation on animation
On how any mayflower can shine even on a boat
Couldn't give us cake even though we slaved and put in
work when we didn't want to, but we had to stay afloat
When she painted this picture, you can tell she wanted
hope

Get In Line

Get in line, I'm the leader, follow me
Wait, don't let me get to three
Or they'll be consequences for sure, you can count on me
I don't even want to hear you humming, be bored
Or let your family see your name on the board
If they can read at all, ha
I can see your future through this crystal ball
You trying to call for your freedom but it's nonexistent
Because of your pigment
That's the reason I'm riding and you're walking
For miles and miles, you'll only hear me talking
So, pick up your feet because I like to hear the chain's
jingle
Being tied up like that makes me glad that I'm single
And free of course, unlike this horse
Because it does everything I say, I'm in charge and he
knows it
Just like yall, I'm the leader because I chose it
So now I got to show it
Put fear into yall heart so there's no fire that could spark up
We don't want little flames because that could mess up the
good time that we're having now
Ain't that right, friend
I'm allowing you to speak now, anything to say man
"we'll -" welp that's all the time we have for now
The mic has been passed back to me
Don't go trailing off, because when I hit you, it hurts me
Don't let me get to three
Or they'll be consequences for sure, you can definitely
count on me

You're Going to Stay Down

People don't understand the weight of this
It's pulling me down while I'm trying to stand up right
So, I'm fighting against gravity but since it has a low sense
of gravity, it's hard to knock down
It's like I'm losing in this continuous fight but I'm getting a
couple hits in
But every time I stop and wait, it adds another weight,
helping gravity bring me down
Look, I'm short but not that short so when I fall, I feel it
Really I'm like a twig hitting the ground, nothing major
But I bounce back like I'm on a trampoline, but it's
something that gravity has already seen
Right back down
Wait, what if I tie this rope to a tree to only climb up but
then I slip and my arm gets stuck
Right back down
Dislocated arm needs to locate the socket so it can go back
to where it came from
Then I realized I didn't have to climb a tree to find my
roots
Now I'm firmly planted creating a low sense of gravity that
even gravity couldn't tackle me
I'm putting my weight down so I'm unison with the weight
now
Wait, am I conforming to the form that they want me to
write now
Sign here, and gravity will take you and put you in a cycle
that you can't get out of
So, I'm going around and around like a Mary go round,
constantly going up and down
I'm at a park I'm not amused by
So, I lay here until the world stops spinning

But I didn't conform, so I'm firmly planted in the ground, grinning
The more gravity and weight pushing me down, the closer
I am to my roots, so I'm winning
Until they push me all the way in the ground, trying to hide me
My roots, my culture, my color, they could never hide we
They try to knock us out like Ronda Rousey
Right back down
The only seats open are on the back of the bus, so I'll stand
Stand my ground since they unrooted me
See that I'm obviously black, I'm always under scrutiny
We're constantly being thrown to the ground for "security" purposes
Right back down
They're still using their weight to hold us
They stole us and our papers, they trying to fold us
With them boulders they're getting bolder
They think they soldiers
Fighting for MAGA, they're getting colder
I'm gonna smack ya, you're getting closer
They got a gun, and I'm getting colder
They shot me back down

Starting Point/You're Better Than Me

"I'm better than you"
You're maybe right but we didn't have the same starting
point
You maybe grew up in a better situation than me
While you used metal, I used plastic cutlery
Open your eyes so you can see
The major difference between you and me, you and I
See, even in schools you had better education
More funding for your school, so your teachers could teach
my teachers
And my teachers would learn something
I learned nothing but math 7th and 8th grade, but my
grades weren't suffering
Eating them school lunches got my stomach bubbling
At least you had access to better food even though you had
to pay
But that was no problem for you because you never had to
pay
Parents always had the finances, but my parents couldn't
stay
For too long, it said so long, astalavista
I'm gone and I'm not coming back, maybe get a pizza
Something cheap that could possibly feed us

What's Your Protest

What's your protest?
My protest is the injustice for the dark earth tones
These injustices of the justice system that is not for us,
where's Fubu because they're
They're adding up more of the stress for us
Subtracting so there are less of us
Taking what is really best for us
Trying to get to the rest of us
They're teaching us a lesson
That we a destined to be great, release the compressions
Remember 2008, release the restrictions

What's your protest?
What do you challenge while you're blessed?
Someone has it better
Someone has it worse
Your color or gender doesn't exclude you
The world around you
Needs you
To truly live you must serve
Not just swerve
Start by liking a Facebook post
That challenges shootings from coast to coast
Tell that young Queen she can be fly
Even more when educated because the limit isn't the sky
Being young and African American
Oh, and a woman
What's your protest?
Young brothers need to protect each other
We're tired of seeing that grieving mother
Not everyone is a front line marcher
But one can't witness the slaughter

And sit back and watch
You have a parent, a brother, a friend, a child
Being affected by this fire burning wild
What's your protest?

By: Tommie and Dennis Stanfield

2 Minutes Left

I would like to thank everyone in this difficult situation
Yall been rocking with me for the last few years, but my
time is coming
I didn't have to check my watch cause my grandfather
sounds like trumpets
This victory lap is not my first
I hit a few fly balls, which caused me to double back
But this time I'm right on track, ready to slide home
I let them say whatever behind my back knowing they dead
wrong
But actions speak louder, so this greatness they really
egged on
A lot done did me dirty but I never cracked under the
pressure
Never reacted, really just had to turn my back
I kind of wish I could rewind, to adjust some decisions that
had some baggage attached
Like when I competed when I shouldn't have
Or that time when I deleted what I should've had
I was mistreated which led me to a different path
And I can say, I'm better off for it
I always drove at my own pace, I never had to floor it
But swerved from lane to lane, trying to get a better view
of what was in front of me
I remember I used to tell her all the time that being in the
present is a luxury
So live luxurious in my company
Our business is always private, no need for the press
release to public just yet
We got to give them some time, that unfortunately isn't in
my favor

I was just searching for the flavor of love that equated to
mine
I tried to do better, for everyone else at least
Better understanding of self didn't start until as of late
And lately, I've been getting back into His word, speaking
through me, using my gift to get better at words
Can't you see the improvement
My movements have been discrete
My love was felt even if it was the first time I had the
pleasure to meet
My heartbeat was the best thing I felt everyday
So, appreciate the little things
Always pursue the little dreams
To build that momentum use your inner wings
Unfortunately, I won't be there to see them grow and you
fly but I know you onto better things
I…

Thank You

I would like to thank God for the ability to be creative.
I would like to thank my family and friends for being an inspiration and a positive light in my life.
I would like to thank my brother Dennis for the contribution.
I would like to thank Caz'Mier for painting the cover.
Lastly, I would like to thank everyone that I have met and had conversations with, yall are the reason for this.

Sun Set

Even when the sun sets
The moon always shines the brightest in the dark

This Journey Isn't Over Yet

This Journey Isn't Over Yet

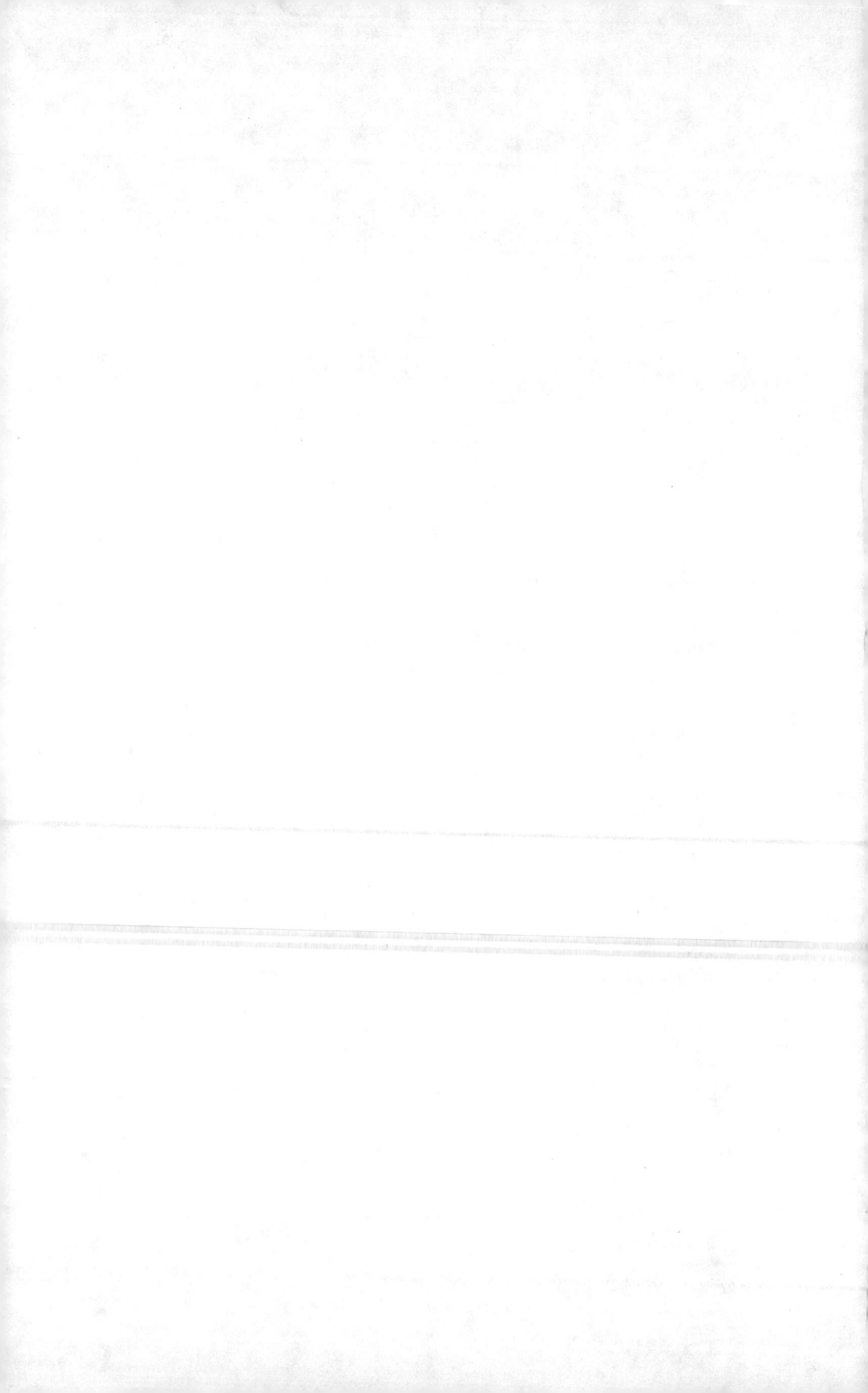